S0-BZE-141

More Best Friend Stories

True Stories About Dogs

A Dolch Classic Basic Reading Book

by Edward W. Dolch and Marguerite P. Dolch

illustrated by Meryl Henderson

The Basic Reading Books

The Basic Reading Books are fun reading books that fill the need for easy-to-read stories for the primary grades. The interest appeal of these true stories will encourage independent reading at the early reading levels.

The stories focus on the 95 Common Nouns and the Dolch 220 Basic Sight Vocabulary. Beyond these simple lists, the books use about two or three new words per page.

This series was prepared under the direction and supervision of Edward W. Dolch, Ph.D.

This revision was prepared under the direction and supervision of Eleanor Dolch LaRoy and the Dolch Family Trust.

SRA/McGraw-Hill

*A Division of The **McGraw·Hill** Companies*

Original version copyright © 1958 by Edward W. Dolch.
Copyright © 1999 by SRA/McGraw-Hill. All rights reserved.
Except as permitted under the United States Copyright Act, no part of this publication may be reproduced or distributed in any form or by any means, or stored in a database or retrieval system without prior written permission from the publisher.

Printed in the United States of America.

Send all inquiries to:
SRA/McGraw-Hill
250 Old Wilson Bridge Road, Suite 310
Worthington, OH 43085

ISBN 0-02-830819-0

2 3 4 5 6 7 8 9 0 QST 04 03 02 01 00 99

Table of Contents

Old Shep
and Young Shep

Dogs that look after sheep are very smart dogs. This is the story of two sheepdogs.

One of these sheepdogs was very old. His owner had got a younger dog to help look after the sheep.

The owner told Old Shep that he was to show Young Shep what he had to do. And the old dog seemed to understand.

Old Shep showed the young dog how to look after the sheep. Every day the sheep had to be taken to where the grass was green. When the sun was going down, the sheep had to be brought home again. When the sheep came into the barnyard, Old Shep seemed to know if one was gone and would go after it.

Sometimes Old Shep and Young Shep took the sheep down the road where the cars were going. But the dogs always kept the sheep on the side of the road. No sheep got hurt or were lost when the dogs were looking after them.

Young Shep was a smart dog and learned very quickly. Soon the old dog began to let the young dog do most of the work.

The dogs were fed every day, but now and then the owner gave each dog a big bone with meat on it. When Young Shep had eaten as much meat off his bone as he wanted, he would bury his bone in the ground.

It is hard work to bury a big bone in the ground. So Old Shep did not bury his bones. But, when Old Shep wanted a bone, he would dig up the bones Young Shep had buried.

What was Young Shep to do?

One day the owner saw Young Shep burying a bone. He was digging a big, big hole. He put his bone in the hole and put a little dirt over the bone.

Then, Young Shep went away. The owner did not know why Young Shep did this.

Soon Young Shep came back. He had an old bone with no meat on it. The dog put the old bone into the hole and covered it with dirt.

Soon the owner saw Old Shep digging in the hole that Young Shep had made. Old Shep came to the old bone, picked it up and carried it away. He did not know that another bone was still down in the hole covered with the dirt.

In this way, Young Shep saved his good bone with the meat on it for himself.

Young Shep was a very smart dog.

Achilles

Achilles was a big, strong dog. He was not afraid to fight any dog. But you had to be careful how you called Achilles.

You had to call Achilles in a kind voice. If you called the big dog in an angry voice, he would not come to you. He would run the other way.

Achilles did not know how strong he was. It was very hard to take a walk with Achilles. His owner always said, "I put Achilles on his leash, and we go for a walk. But Achilles does not walk with me. I go where Achilles wants to go."

If Achilles wanted to go across the street, he just went across the street. He was so strong that his owner could not hold him back. And you could never scold Achilles, or he would just run away from you.

One day Achilles and his owner were going for a walk. Achilles was walking along very slowly.

Suddenly, Achilles saw across the street a little dog barking at a young man. Away went Achilles. He wanted to see this very little dog who was barking so much.

Achilles pulled his owner across the street so fast that she fell down. She let go of the leash. And she was very angry.

"Achilles, you bad dog! Come here!" said the owner.

Away went Achilles down the street as fast as he could go.

The young man said, "I will get your dog for you." And he ran down the street as fast as he could go.

The owner ran down the street as fast as she could go, calling, "Achilles, Achilles."

Some little boys who were playing in the street saw her. They ran on down the street after her as fast as they could go to see what was happening.

A police officer in the street saw the young man coming so fast, with the lady running after him. The police officer stopped the young man and wanted to know what was the matter.

The lady came up just then and told the police officer that they were all trying to catch Achilles, the big dog. So the police officer went with them.

Away went the young man and the police officer and the owner and the little boys down the street calling, "Achilles, Achilles."

Achilles had been running away, but he saw another dog. He did not like this dog, and he stopped and growled. The other dog growled too. And all at once there was a dog fight.

Just then, the young man and the police officer and the owner and the little boys came up.

The owner knew that Achilles did not know how strong he was. He could hurt the other dog very badly.

The young man and the police officer were trying to get Achilles away from the dog. But Achilles would not stop fighting.

Then, the owner went up to the two fighting dogs. Her voice was very kind.

"Achilles, my dear Achilles," she said. "Come, my little pet. Good Achilles. Please come to me!"

Everyone stopped. Everyone looked. They all started to laugh. They had never seen anyone try to stop a dog fight like that.

But Achilles heard his owner. She was calling him "Good dog." Her voice was very kind.

Achilles always thought of himself as a very "good dog." He let go of the other dog and went to his owner right away.

Almo

Almo was a Seeing-Eye dog. He had been trained to look after his owner, who was blind. When the owner left the house, Almo went with him. He kept his owner on the sidewalk. He took his owner across streets. He took care of his owner at all times.

Almo and his owner and the owner's wife were staying on the top floor of a small hotel. They were resting in the afternoon, because that night the owner was to give a talk about the work of Seeing-Eye dogs.

Almo could not keep still. The dog walked up and down the room. Then, he came to the side of his owner's bed and put his cold nose on the owner's face.

The owner knew that something was the matter. He put the harness on Almo and took him into the hall. Everything seemed to be all right.

The owner told Almo to go back to the room. Almo did not want to go back. But he obeyed.

The owner started to take the harness off Almo, but Almo barked and barked and pushed his owner toward the door. The owner did not know what to do.

At last, the owner called his wife who had been sleeping. His wife could see and find out what was the matter.

Now all three went out into the hall. The owner smelled smoke at once.

His wife said, "The hall is full of smoke. I cannot see anything."

The owner could hardly breathe because of the smoke. He heard people calling, "Fire! Fire!" He knew that his wife's eyes could not help. So he called to Almo and said, "To the door outside."

The dog went down the hall through the smoke. The owner had hold of Almos's harness, and the wife had hold of the owner's arm.

Suddenly Almo stopped and barked. The owner put out his hand. They had come to a window.

"Almo has brought us to the fire escape," he said to his wife. He opened the window.

The owner wanted Almo to go out first. "Outside," he said. But Almo would not go. Then the owner knew that Almo would not leave him. So the owner climbed through the window and out on the part of the fire escape in front of the window. Almo went with him. Then, the wife climbed out.

Then, they could breathe.

The fire escape went down to a roof. Firefighters were on the roof. They were calling to the people on the fire escape.

The owner climbed down the fire escape. It did not go all the way to the roof. So when the owner came to the end of it, he fell the rest of the way. But he was not hurt.

Firefighters went up the fire escape and got the owner's wife. Almo was left up on the fire escape all by himself.

The owner's wife knew that Almo could not come down the fire escape. So

she told two firefighters how to pick up
the big dog.

"Put one arm under him just back of
his front legs. Put another arm under
him at his back legs. Then, you can carry
him without hurting him."

A firefighter went up the fire escape.
He picked up Almo and carried him
down to the roof.

The firefighters were calling from the ground for the people to get off the roof near the fire. So the firefighters took the owner and his wife and Almo across the roofs to where they would be away from the fire.

The owner and his wife were saved, because Almo found his way through the smoke to a window where the fire escape was.

The Captain's Dog

The "Elsie," a big ship, was carrying many men, women, and children. A storm was blowing up at sea. Then, something broke in the ship. The captain could not steer the ship.

The high winds blew the ship toward the shore. Near the shore were great rocks that would break the ship to pieces. Everyone on the ship would be lost.

On the shore, people stood in the wind and rain. The ship was not far from the shore. But no one could get out to the ship, because the waves were too high.

The people on the shore got a big gun that fired a big ball with a rope on it. If they could shoot the ball over the ship, the people on the ship could get the rope. Then, they could pull the rope and get hold of a bigger rope that was tied to it. They could tie the big rope to the ship. Then, a basket could be pulled out to the ship to take off people.

Again, the people on the shore fired the gun. But the wind was blowing so hard that they could not get the big ball to go over the ship. The rocks and the high waves were beginning to break up the ship.

The captain of the "Elsie" had a big black dog that always was with him. The dog seemed to know that something was happening to the ship. He ran up and down and barked and barked. The captain had a thought.

"Come here," said the captain to the big dog. "Maybe you can save us. A person cannot get through those waves. Maybe a dog can."

The captain tied a rope to the dog's collar. Then he said, "Swim to the shore, boy. Swim to the shore."

The big dog jumped into the water. The big waves pushed him this way and that. But he kept on swimming.

The people on the ship stood and watched the dog. The people on the shore saw the dog, too. They stood and watched.

Sometimes the people could see the big black head of the dog as he was swimming in the water. Sometimes the waves would break over the head of the dog, and he would be gone. But, then, he would come up again, still swimming.

As the big dog got near the shore, the people were afraid that he would be thrown on the rocks and be killed.

Some people on the shore tried to get out into the water to help the dog. But the waves drove them back. As the dog got nearer to the shore, the people saw that he was so tired that he could hardly swim. Then, a big wave broke over his head, and he went down.

The people on the shore went again into the water to save the dog. They got to him. They pulled him to the shore. The big dog lay on the shore, trying to breathe.

The men on the shore quickly took the rope from the dog's collar. They tied a big rope onto the end of it. And the captain and his men pulled and pulled and got the big rope to the ship. It did not take long to get the big basket going from the ship to the shore. It was blown by the winds, but it went right over the great high waves. The basket got all of the men, women, and children to the shore.

The big black dog had saved them.

Nick, the Sheepdog

Nick was a black sheepdog. He was little for a dog that drives sheep, but he would be called a big dog if he were a pet in town. Nick helped his owner and the other sheepdog, Rock, herd sheep out in the mountains of Arizona.

One day, the owner bought a big herd of sheep. He wanted to take the sheep up into the hills where there was good grass. The sheep would grow and grow. Later on, the owner could sell them for more money.

After the owner bought the sheep, he found there were goats in with the sheep. The owner had not bought the goats. So the goats had to be taken out of the herd of sheep.

This work was done by Nick and Rock. They picked out the goats one at a time. They ran the goats through a gate into another yard. Soon the goats were all out.

Then, the dogs began to drive the herd of sheep. For a long day, the herd was driven up into the hills of Arizona.

The owner was heading for a water hole, because sheep cannot go too long without water to drink. When they got to the water hole, there was no water in it.

While the herd was resting, some of the sheep smelled water. Five of them started off toward the smell of water. They left the rest of the herd and headed right for a river.

Nick started out after the five sheep, but the sheep got to the river first.

The river was full of water and was going fast. The fast water was carrying the sheep down the river. One sheep got out on a rock that was in the river. Nick knew that the sheep would just stay there. So Nick knew that he must swim out to the rock. He climbed the rock and pushed the sheep off of it.

Then, Nick jumped into the river again after the sheep. He got it out of the water. He drove all five away from the river.

This time, the five sheep went up a deep canyon with steep sides. They could not climb the sides. They got up on some rocks and could not turn around. They did not know how to go on, and they did not know enough to go back.

Nick had to climb up on the rocks. He got through the sheep and got ahead of them. Then, he made them turn around. Nick got the sheep to go down from the rocks.

At last Nick saw a place where they could get out of the canyon. He drove the five sheep up this place. Now they were out of the canyon. Nick drove them toward the grass higher up.

The sheep came to another deep canyon that had a bridge across it. But there was a gate. Nick knew this bridge. He had got sheep over it before. But the owner was not there to open the gate. So Nick opened the gate himself. He took the end of the gate with his teeth. Then, he pulled it back. The sheep went over the bridge.

As Nick drove the sheep along, they came to some high rocks. From the top of the rocks, a mountain lion jumped down on one of the sheep. The others ran away. But Nick ran up and barked and barked.

The mountain lion knew that a barking dog meant more dogs and men with guns. The mountain lion turned and ran. The sheep that the lion had jumped down on was hurt and could not keep up with the other sheep.

Nick got four of the sheep back to the owner and the herd. But he knew one was left behind. So he went back to get it. It was the sheep that had been hurt by the lion. Nick had to bite the sheep again and again to keep it going. At last he got that sheep back to the herd.

The owner gave Nick some food. He told Nick he was a good dog. But Nick just did what any good sheepdog knew had to be done. Nick knew that his owner's sheep must be kept together.

Snowbird

Two men named Luke and Beaver lived in Alaska. They were fur trappers. In the winter they went to their traps over the snow on snowshoes. The snow was very deep, but the snowshoes let the men walk right on top of the snow.

One evening Luke and Beaver were going back to their camp. The snow came down so hard that they could hardly see to find their way.

Suddenly, the men heard a dog crying. They knew that something was not right. They ran to where the cry came from and found that a big wolf was fighting a black dog. Luke chased the wolf away, but the wolf had hurt the dog very badly.

When the men got to the dog, they found that it was a mother dog. She was hurt very badly, but she knew that the men were friends. She took them to where there were two puppies. One puppy was white and one puppy was black.

The mother had been fighting to save her puppies from the wolf. But she knew that the men were friends, and the puppies would be taken care of. She lay down in the snow, and she was so badly hurt that soon she died.

Luke and Beaver took the puppies to their camp. The puppies were so small that their eyes were not open. The men had some milk, and they fed the puppies. They kept the puppies very warm.

Day by day, the puppies grew and grew. The white puppy was called Snowbird. The black puppy was called Blacky. Both of the big trappers loved the dogs. They loved to play with Snowbird and Blacky. They were very happy to have the puppies.

The two men had to do their work every day. They had to go and see their traps. They had to move from one camp to another. It was hard to take good care of the puppies and to feed them and keep them warm.

Luke and Beaver had a small sled that they pulled themselves. But they could not put the puppies on the sled. The puppies would be too cold. So the men made little hammocks for the puppies. They hung these hammocks under their coats.

Luke carried Snowbird and Beaver carried Blacky. Each man had a puppy in a hammock in front of him, under his coat. The coat would keep the puppy warm and would keep the puppy from putting its head out and getting it cold.

At last the men got to the camp, which was an Inuit village. The Inuits came out to see the puppies. Snowbird was all white, with blue eyes. Blacky was all black with big brown eyes. The Inuits looked and looked at them.

Snowbird and Blacky grew to be big strong dogs. Luke and Beaver taught them to pull a sled. In Alaska at that time, the only way to get from place to place in the winter was by sled. A sled pulled by dogs could go over snow, through woods, and along rivers.

Luke and Beaver made a small sled that was pulled only by their two dogs. But most sleds were larger. Some men would make big sleds that had many dogs to pull them over the snow. Good sled dogs would bring a lot of money.

One day, Luke and Beaver thought that they would go over the mountains to find the Yukon River. They were told they could not do it, but they wanted to try. So they started.

For many days the two men and their sled with their two dogs went higher and higher into the mountains. The wind blew and blew. They got very tired. Their food was all gone. The way was much longer than the men had thought. Would they die in the mountains?

Snowbird went on and on, but Blacky was not strong enough. He could not go on pulling the sled. He could not go on without food. And so he died right up near the top of the mountains.

The sled, pulled now by Snowbird alone, went on and on. The men ran beside it. At last they began to go down. The men caught a rabbit and ate it. They gave Snowbird his part. Then, they found more food. And at last they could get out of the wind and rest.

After a long time the men and the dog got to the Yukon River. There were people who gave them food.

This has been the story of how Snowbird grew up and became a great sled dog. But Snowbird's name was changed. The next story will tell you about Snowbird when his name was changed to Sandy.

Sandy

Big Mike was a man who took the letters and packages from one village in Alaska to another. He had many fine sled dogs. A sled pulled by dogs was the only way you could go from place to place over ice and snow in winter.

As soon as Big Mike saw Snowbird he wanted to buy him. He said he would give Luke a lot of money for his big dog with blue eyes. But Luke would not sell Snowbird.

Then Luke and Beaver found they had to leave Alaska for a time. They had to leave to sell their furs. So they said that they would not sell Snowbird to Big Mike, but they would let him keep Snowbird for them while they were gone.

Big Mike had to say that he would be very good to Snowbird.

Big Mike changed Snowbird's name to Sandy because the big dog's coat was turning a light yellow. And "Sandy" was a much better name to call out when he called to his dogs as they pulled the sled.

Sandy was so big and strong that he was made the lead dog of Big Mike's team of sled dogs. The lead dog has to be very smart. He has to pick the way to go because there are no roads over the snow. The lead dog has to keep all the other dogs pulling as they go after him.

Then, too, the lead dog has to keep the other dogs from fighting. Sandy was very big and strong, but he did not like to fight. When two of the sled dogs would start to fight, Sandy would watch them. Then, just at the right time, he would run at them and knock them both over. They would be so surprised that they would stop fighting.

There was one time when Sandy would not obey Big Mike.

It was almost the time of the "long night" when the sun hardly comes up at all. Big Mike was going across the hills to a village. It was a new trail for the man and his team of sled dogs.

It was almost dark when Sandy suddenly stopped and sat down. The dogs and sled stopped behind him.

"Mush," cried Big Mike. "Mush" means to go ahead. But Sandy would not move.

The dogs had been going all day, and Big Mike thought that maybe the dogs were too tired. So Big Mike stopped for the night. He fed the dogs and camped right there.

In the morning, it was time to start, but it was still very dark. Big Mike wanted to get going on his way. He harnessed the dogs.

"Mush," cried Big Mike. But Sandy would not move. He stood still. He would not go on.

Big Mike was very angry. This was the first time that Sandy had not obeyed him.

"Mush," cried Big Mike again. But Sandy did not move.

Then, Big Mike got out of the sled. It was so dark that he could hardly see Sandy at the head of the team of dogs. But Big Mike went up to where Sandy stood in the snow.

Just as Big Mike got to Sandy, his feet went from under him. He started to go down a steep hill that he had not seen.

Sandy jumped and got hold of Big Mike's coat with his teeth. He pulled back, and all the other dogs pulled back. They all seemed to know that they could all go down over the hill.

The dogs pulled and pulled. Slowly Big Mike got back up the steep hill. He got to his feet.

After that, Big Mike always trusted Sandy. Sandy was a good sled dog leader.

The Race

Big Mike and his dog team had to go to Nome. In Nome, Big Mike found that there was going to be a big race. The best dogs from all over Alaska had been brought to Nome for the race.

One of the men who was to have a team in the race was John Johnson, who was called the Iron Man because he was so strong. As soon as Johnson saw Sandy in Big Mike's team, he wanted to buy Sandy to be his lead dog in the race.

"Sandy is not my dog," said Big Mike. "I cannot sell him."

"I must have Sandy as my lead dog in the big race," said Johnson. "I will take good care of him. If you let me have him just for the race, I will take care of all your dogs while you are in Nome."

At last, Big Mike let Johnson have Sandy to be his lead dog in the race.

The race was to be from Nome to a town called Candle and then back to Nome. It was 408 miles in all. And there were to be eight teams in the race.

The day of the race, a blizzard began. But Sandy had gone through many blizzards. Johnson's team was to go first. This was not good, because the first team had to make the trail that the others could follow. But Johnson was not afraid. He was sure that he could keep ahead of the others.

"Mush," called Johnson, the Iron Man, and away the dogs went. On and on through the blizzard. On and on.

The race began at ten in the morning and the dogs ran all that day. In the afternoon, they had gone over 70 miles. Johnson let the dogs rest and fed them. Then, they went on again through the snow. No one had caught up with them.

All night long the dogs kept going.
Every few hours they would rest a few
minutes. Johnson would go along the
team and talk to each dog, calling it by
name. He would look at their feet to be
sure they were not hurt.

Sandy seemed to know that every dog must run as fast as he could and keep on going. The dogs ran all the next day. They rested now and then and were given something to eat. In the afternoon, they got to Candle ahead of all the other teams. But they had to have some rest.

Johnson, the Iron Man, went to sleep for four hours. When he woke up, he found that another team had come to Candle and had started back.

But Johnson took time to take good care of his dogs and talk to them. He fed them and then harnessed them to the sled. But while Johnson did this, three more dog teams had got to Candle and had started back ahead of them.

When they were ready, "Mush," called the Iron Man, and they started off on the trail to Nome. This time they could follow the track of the other teams. But Johnson's team could not come up behind another team and go by them. If they did this, the dogs would be sure to have a great fight. So when Johnson knew that a team was ahead of his, he told Sandy to make a new trail so that they could get around the other team and get ahead of them. This made the trail longer.

At last, Johnson, the Iron Man, knew that he was ahead of all the other teams. Now they must keep ahead of them. All day and all night the dogs had run with just a few stops to rest and eat. The dogs were very tired. The Iron Man, who was so strong, was very tired, too.

A blizzard was blowing harder and harder. Johnson knew if he stopped again, the dogs were so tired that they would all go to sleep and not want to go on.

Sandy seemed to understand. He kept going. The Iron Man talked to his dogs. He could hardly see them because his eyes were almost covered with snow.

Sandy ran on and on. The ice on the trail had cut his feet. He left red spots on the snow as he ran on and on.

Three days after they had started, the Iron Man and his team of dogs got back to Nome ahead of all the others. They had won the race.

Sandy, the lead dog, was now the most famous dog in Alaska. The papers told the story of the race. Luke, who had just come back, was very happy. His dog came back to him, and they were together again.

a
about
Achilles
across
afraid
after
afternoon
again
ahead
Alaska
all
Almo
Almo's
almost
alone
along
always
an
and
angry
another
any
anyone
anything
are
Arizona
arm
around
as
at
ate
away
back
bad
badly
ball
barked

barking
barnyard
basket
be
Beaver
became
because
bed
been
before
began
beginning
behind
beside
best
better
big
bigger
bit
bite
black
Blacky
blew
blind
blizzard
blizzards
blowing
blown
blue
bone
bones
both
bought
boy
boys
break
breathe

bridge
bring
broke
brought
brown
buried
bury
burying
but
buy
by
call
called
calling
came
camp
camped
can
candle
cannot
canyon
captain
captain's
care
careful
carried
carry
carrying
cars
catch
caught
changed
chased
children
climb
climbed
coat

coats
cold
collar
come
comes
coming
could
covered
cried
cry
crying
cut
dark
day
days
dear
deep
did
die
died
dig
digging
dirt
do
does
dog
dogs
dog's
done
door
down
drink
drive
driven
drives
drove
each

eat	four
eaten	friends
eight	from
Elsie	front
end	full
enough	fur
escape	furs
evening	gate
every	gave
everyone	get
everything	getting
eye	give
eyes	given
face	go
famous	goats
far	going
fast	gone
fed	good
feed	got
feet	grass
fell	great
few	green
fight	grew
fighting	ground
find	grow
fine	growled
fire	gun
fired	guns
firefighter	had
firefighters	hall
first	hammock
five	hammocks
floor	hand
follow	happening
food	happy
for	hard
found	harder

hardly	Inuit
harness	Inuits
harnessed	Iron Man
has	is
have	it
he	its
head	John
headed	Johnson
heading	Johnson's
heard	jumped
help	just
helped	keep
her	kept
herd	killed
here	kind
high	knew
higher	knock
hill	know
hills	lady
him	larger
himself	last
his	later
hold	laugh
hole	lay
home	lead
hotel	leader
hours	learned
house	leash
how	leave
hung	left
hurt	legs
hurting	let
I	letters
ice	light
if	like
in	lion
into	little

lived	my
long	name
longer	named
look	near
looked	nearer
looking	never
lost	new
lot	next
loved	Nick
Luke	night
made	no
make	Nome
man	nose
many	not
matter	now
maybe	obey
me	obeyed
means	of
meant	off
meat	officer
men	old
Mike	on
Mike's	once
miles	one
milk	only
minutes	open
money	opened
more	or
morning	other
most	others
mother	out
mountain	outside
mountains	over
move	owner
much	owner's
mush	packages
must	papers

part	roof
people	roofs
person	room
pet	rope
pick	run
picked	running
pieces	said
place	Sandy
play	Sandy's
playing	sat
please	save
police	saved
pull	saw
pulled	say
pulling	scold
puppies	sea
puppy	see
pushed	seeing
put	Seeing-Eye
putting	seemed
quickly	seen
rabbit	sell
race	she
rain	sheep
ran	sheepdog
ready	sheepdogs
red	Shep
rest	ship
rested	shoot
resting	shore
right	show
river	showed
rivers	side
road	sides
roads	sidewalk
rock	sled
rocks	sleds

sleep
sleeping
slowly
small
smart
smell
smelled
smoke
snow
Snowbird
Snowbird's
snowing
snowshoes
so
some
something
sometimes
soon
spots
start
started
stay
staying
steep
steer
still
stood
stop
stopped
stops
storm
story
street
streets
strong
suddenly
sun

sure
surprised
swim
swimming
take
taken
talk
talked
taught
team
teams
teeth
tell
ten
than
that
the
their
them
themselves
then
there
these
they
this
those
thought
three
through
thrown
tie
tied
time
times
tired
to
together

told	wave
too	waves
took	way
top	we
toward	went
town	were
track	what
trail	when
trained	where
trappers	which
traps	while
tried	white
trusted	who
try	why
trying	wife
turn	wife's
turned	will
turning	wind
two	window
under	winds
understand	winter
up	with
us	without
very	woke
village	wolf
voice	women
walk	won
walked	woods
walking	work
want	would
wanted	yard
wants	yellow
warm	you
was	young
watch	younger
watched	your
water	Yukon River